Emotive

Reflex Method

Emotive Reflex Method

Your Wellness Empowerment System

Scott Donat

What people are saying about Scott Donat, The FootGuy

The ERM system is the perfect complement for anyone that is committed to a holistic approach for their healing process.

Dr. Ruth M. Rodriguez, D.O.

Emotive Reflex Method is a great tool for both body workers and laypeople to help in releasing and resolving the source of health issues.

Julie Rattelmueller, LMT, Denver, CO

The tools presented here are an amazing compliment to my practice and my own personal self-care regiment. This book is a must read for those looking to add an edge to their wellness business.

Rev. Veronica Lightning Horse Perez, Denver, CO

Every reflexology session I have had with Scott has been a blessing. Along with all the techniques he shares, he always adds the most important ingredients to all sessions: an open heart and sense of gratitude, and a true desire that we heal and enjoy our lives to the fullest.

Kathleen Long, Rockledge, FL

I am one of the lucky ones who have had the pleasure of having Scott work on my feet. He combines his knowledge of the body with an intuitive knowledge of the spirit. Think mind-body-spirit connection!

Sue Maynard Diez, Cape Canaveral, FL

Scott's the real deal! This is his passion. He enjoys making people feel well, he knows what he's doing, he connects physically and energetically, and it shows!

Jahn Dussich, Rockledge, FL

Scott is more than just a "FootGuy"; he supports his clients on many levels. The depth of emotional and spiritual intuition combined with his knowledge and skill in the study of reflexology create a healing space that tickles the spirit and swaddles the soul. To be in his presence for any session work is to meet joy, authenticity, and love as the mirror we need to invoke and inspire healing, transformation, and growth.

Shannon Plummer, Rockledge, FL

Intuitive, knowledgeable, and gifted - Scott is all of these things and more. An appointment involves attention to all bodies: mental, emotional, spiritual, and physical. Scott brings to the table a dynamic and deep tool box which allows him to hone in and sense what each client needs. The result is a beautiful space that allows for deep and powerful healing on all levels.

Tolly Tucker, LMT

This book and course bring together Scott's innate wisdom of healing through the use of reflexology, oils, and eastern philosophies. As an acupuncturist, I appreciate the depth of the sublime tool that Scott shares with other healers. Through this book you can deepen your skills and add to your toolbox to help others.

Terry Treece, L.Ac, Gate of Hope Acupuncture

This book is dedicated to my late wife, Kathryn S. Donat, A.P., the first person to acknowledge the healer in me, and to my mentor, Art Sellers, for empowering me to become that healer.

Table of Contents

Acknowledgements

My heartfelt gratitude goes to Mark Pasqualino for helping me envision The FootGuy and ERM, to Patricia Krause for teaching me the magic of tuning forks, and to Tammy Ecker for introducing me to essential oils. Diana Huntress has been my mentor, accountability coach, and manuscript editor; this book would not have come to fruition without her support. Betty Lynne Bolt Leary and Barbara Bolt also provided exceptional editing. Keith Leon, Babypie Publishing, coached me through the maze of producing and releasing a book. Shannon Procise helped me navigate the intricacies of being a small business, and Robert Raymond from Achieve Systems made my business aspirations come alive.

I will forever be grateful to Dwight "The Footman" Byers (1929 – 2020) for being my teacher and guide into the amazing world of reflexology.

A very special thank you goes to my wife, Becky Bolt, for believing in me and transcribing my scattered thoughts and words to create this work. I am also grateful to our daughters Amberline Chapple, Hannah Rhodes, Melissa Qualls, and Courtney Donat, and their families, for being my motivation to share wellness and healing with the world.

Foreword

I am a retired Navy Captain with a 30-year career in logistics. I had touched on reflexology and read about other modalities over the years, but my life was basically very structured and traditional. I met Scott five years ago when I responded to a post in a shop window offering mobile reflexology.

When a very tall, hippie reflexologist appeared at my door, I thought I had gone through a time-warp. He wore a tie-dyed t-shirt and used the word "groovy" in at least every third sentence. But he was a fantastic reflexologist, so I continued to see him and introduce his work to my friends and family.

As time went on, we became friends and he told me about his expanding interest in areas that complemented his reflexology work. He would experiment with his oils, spheres, and tuning forks on my feet, developing his knowledge and perfecting his technique. But he still used "groovy" in every third sentence and wore tie-dyed t-shirts. Our relationship was very frank and open. We knew we could talk without the other taking offense, no matter what was said. When we discussed his business ideas, either my logistics background or my age/gender perspective would often provide a completely different outlook. It was clear that he wanted to be more than he was, but he was not getting there.

One day I said to him, "Scott, if you want to be a very good hippie reflexologist, then I am happy to have you come here and be just that. But if you want to be more, you have to show up as the person that you want to be. You can't just continue to be as you are and expect more to happen for you." Starting that day, everything changed, as he seriously worked toward becoming the healing professional that he is today.

What sets Scott apart from most healers is that he connects both physically and energetically with a client. His knowledge of how emotions affect and manifest in the body enhances his ability to bring about meaningful change in a short session. He has a passion for wellness, but recognizes that he cannot make someone well by his actions alone. That is why he has written this book - to empower people to use his tools and techniques to move themselves ahead to a state of wellness. Through this book, Scott will teach you how to show up as the WELL person that you want to be.

Oh, by the way, he still says "groovy" every few months, just to make me laugh.

Captain Diana Huntress, SC, USN, retired

Introduction

The FootGuy, a mobile reflexology business located in central Florida, was founded in 2014 and incorporated in 2015. However, it was conceived some 20 years earlier while a friend and I sat on my back porch reminiscing about growing up in the northeast. We started talking about the old-time knife sharpener who would walk through our neighborhoods pulling his cart behind him, ringing a brass bell. Once enough folks had gathered at the end of their driveways, he would stop and flip his cart around to make a mobile workspace, complete with a seat and sharpening stone. Each family brought their shears, knives, and lawn mower blades and he worked until everyone's tools were sharp. Then he would flip his seat and sharpening stone back around, pack his cart, and be off, ringing his bell, into the next neighborhood. It was a brilliant business model. My friend and I sat for hours dreaming up carts and stools and chairs that would allow me, as a reflexologist, to mimic the knife sharpener's mobility. This was also when the name FootGuy was born.

At the time, I was the co-owner of an alternative health care and acupuncture center. Besides being the certified reflexologist, I was also responsible for the intake and preliminary diagnostic testing of incoming clients. I spent many hours researching disease and contraindications that were presented by our patients, and looked for holistic alternatives for treatments.

Fifteen years passed, as did lots of water under the bridges of my life, but in 2014, I began providing mobile reflexology all over Brevard County, Florida, as the Foot-Guy, LLC. During my second year in business, as my practice grew, I rediscovered a truth that I had known but forgotten: reflexology can be painful. Another friend who was well versed in the applications of essential oils suggested that oils might help reduce pain levels and potentially resolve physical issues. I also noticed another consistent similarity among my clients and that was emotion. Anger, sadness, rage, resentment, grief, and more were commonplace occurrences during sessions. Because our physical ailments have an underlying emotional component, I could correlate the emotional responses elicited by the reflexology to the corresponding body parts, helping clients unravel the full story of their negative health patterns.

In an effective FootGuy session, the cause of the client's discomfort is identified with reflexology assisted by essential oils and is acknowledged and owned emotionally by the client. The next step is to stabilize the energy and regain balance. I learned during sessions that there were two kinds of pain responses: a sharp and shooting pain that indicated excess energy, or a dull and achy pain that indicated an energy deficiency. Which kind of pain presented told me about the nature of the imbalances in the reflexes and how it manifested in the client's physical and emotional bodies. The question became how to augment or release energy based on the client's indications.

Once again, another friend, my tuning fork master trainer and vibrational teacher, helped me find the answer. I shared with her how an acupuncture needle is manipulated by the acupuncturist. The direction that the needle is twisted upon insertion determines whether qi (energy) is added or diminished. Upon hearing that, she jumped up, went to her storage closet, and returned with two tuning forks: the Moon (210.42 mhz) and the Sun (126.22 mhz). The sharp and shooting pain response indicating excess energy can be treated with the Moon tuning fork to diminish qi levels in that reflex. The dull and achy response indicating a qi deficiency requires the application of the Sun tuning fork. Problem solved!

The last piece of the FootGuy process to come together was Wellness Spheres, and they went through a two-year evolution to achieve their present form. Early in my practice, I used golf balls, tennis balls, and crystal spheres to finish off a session. Clients loved these rolling tools for no other reason than they felt really good on their feet. The final impetus behind the creation of Wellness Spheres occurred when I was working in a client's upscale home, closing a session with a beautiful 45 mm crystal sphere. I lost control of it and the sphere fell to the tile floor, making a loud cracking sound. Unfortunately, it was not the crystal that cracked, it was the recently installed, gorgeous Mexican tile. I replaced the tile, retired the crystal spheres, and created a wooden ball with my company logo on it that fit in the palm of my hand. After using it on myself and my family, I quickly realized the possibilities and Wellness Spheres were born. They are

a set of four attractive, oil-infused wooden balls of varying sizes. The first set was huge and almost impossible to
work with on the feet. Each successive incarnation was
smaller until I arrived at their present sizes of ½ inch,
¾ inch, 1 inch, and 1 ¼ inch. As a practitioner, the vari-
able sizes allow me to work on all of the foot's nooks,
crannies, and flat spaces. Wellness Spheres are also the
perfect take-home self-care tool because they are easy to
use and sit on a nice-looking stand so the Spheres can
remain out and ready for use.

The FootGuy is the core and foundation of the Emotive Reflex Method (ERM), offering ancient healing to a
modern world. Combining reflexology, essential oils,
tuning forks, and Wellness Spheres with the founda-
tional power and wisdom of the emotional body, ERM
is a holistic wellness empowerment system. I developed
ERM in 2018 and it is offered as both hands-on and online training.

This book is a more in-depth exploration of the
concepts taught within the ERM training. Where did
the modalities originate, what theories or ideas were
at their foundations, and how did they evolve into the
ERM system? I wrote the book with two audiences in
mind: laypeople and professional body workers. For the
layperson, attending the ERM training would be beneficial, but not a necessity. This book will acquaint you
with the foot maps that are the basis of reflexology and
Wellness Spheres, the most important ERM self-care tool
for laypeople. Once you have read the book, you will
feel comfortable and be competent to care for yourself

and your family. For the practitioner, attending the ERM training is strongly suggested. This book provides further insight into the purpose and intention behind each technique taught and tool used in the ERM class. It will help you create an integrative system that includes caring for your clients and also teaching them to care for themselves. You will have choices: ERM can become your primary practice, a fully integrated piece of your existing practice, or a stand-alone offering within your practice. You do not have to work hard and become an expert in all of the modalities within ERM to benefit greatly from it.

I have developed an enjoyable and meaningful practice and am pleased to teach ERM to you. By following your heart (or in this case, your feet), and with a bit of effort, you can give yourself, your family, and/ or your clients the gift of wellness. So welcome, and let's get started by dividing this system into its working parts.

Chapter One

History of ERM

What is Emotive Reflex Method (ERM)?

Emotive - arousing, or able to arouse, intense feelings

Reflex - a response in a part of the body to stimulation of a corresponding point on the feet or hands

Method - a systematic or established procedure for accomplishing or approaching something

The FootGuy, my mobile reflexology business, originated in 2014 and was the natural, spontaneous result of my 16 years of experience as a traditional reflexologist and the 22 years I had been facilitating an emotional breakthrough workshop called The Way Through Experience. In 2018, I developed a course to teach people the FootGuy methodology, but wanted a more broad-based title than FootGuy, and the name ERM was born. It is the combination of five healing modalities that creates a powerful and effective wellness system. The ancient art of reflexology, enhanced with essential oils, is used to discover and identify energy blockages in the body. Next, the emotional causes of the blockages are examined so the client can identify and acknowledge personal patterns that contribute to the physical ailments. It became crystal clear to me that the connection between the physical body and the emotions is extremely powerful, and that true wellness cannot be achieved without addressing both components. The final stage of ERM is to use the modern tools of tuning forks and Wellness Spheres to balance the energy, resulting in relief and wellness. The tagline for ERM and The FootGuy is Ancient Healing for a Modern World.

Reflexology is the core of the discovery portion of ERM; basic reflexology techniques are used to identify weaknesses and blockages present throughout the body. It is not necessary for a layperson or an ERM practitioner to become a reflexologist, but an understanding of how and why reflexology works, and the ability to perform a few simple techniques are necessary to be successful.

The other part of the ancient component of ERM is the integration of essential oils with reflexology to help pinpoint the deeper nature and structure of the body's imbalances. Applying the right oil to the feet at the right time allows greater stimulation of a reflex with less discomfort to the client. Oils can also be used to provide a pleasant ending to a treatment session. Essential oils are fast becoming a modern phenomenon. However, they have their origins in the tinctures and reductions of ancient times. The use of essential oils for everything from pain relief to repairing bone and muscle damage, to emotional, mental, and spiritual applications has been occurring for thousands of years. Current technology allows us to look at the chemical and molecular structures of essential oils, further enhancing our understanding and their value.

Identifying the physical indicators of blockages only addresses the symptoms of dis-ease and not the root causes. When emotional issues are not confronted, they can become physically debilitating. Emotional awareness is what sets ERM apart from other wellness systems. By facilitating the client's ownership of the destructive emotions that contributed to the physical imbalances, authentic deep release that leads to healing can be achieved. The provider must develop empathy so that the desired level of trust and vulnerability with the client can be attained. Additionally, providers must be comfortable expressing their own emotions if they expect to engender authentic emotion from others.

Modern tools are used to release the blockages discovered using reflexology, essential oils, and emotional awareness. The vibrational power of tuning forks impacts a single reflex by infusing or diffusing energy. The rhythmic flow of Wellness Spheres impacts the entire body through stimulation of all of the reflexes on the bottoms of the feet. These two tools, alone or in combination, create the atmosphere for profound physical and emotional release that will lead to balance (Figure 1).

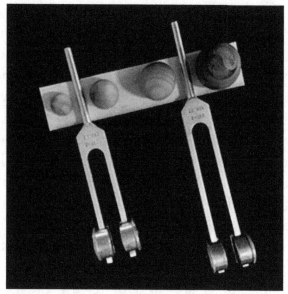

Figure 1. Tuning forks and Wellness Spheres.

ERM was developed to be a holistic system that addresses the physical and emotional causes of imbalance, pain, and dis-ease. Each of the tools incorporated in the ERM system serves a specific purpose and contributes to the final goal of wellness.

Chapter Two

Reflexology

History

Reflexology was documented more than 6,000 years ago in Asia and again in 2,500 B.C. in Egypt, and has been passed down through spoken tradition in indigenous cultures for many generations. It is believed that reflexology was introduced into Europe in the early 1300s by Marco Polo when he translated into Italian a handwritten book about massage that he brought back from Asia. In 1582, two doctors practicing in Italy, Adamus and Atatis, published the book, *Zone Therapy*, which was the precursor to modern-day reflexology. In *Zone Therapy*, the entire body was divided laterally from the midline out on the feet (Figure 1), and pain within a body zone could be treated by putting pressure on distal points within the same zone.

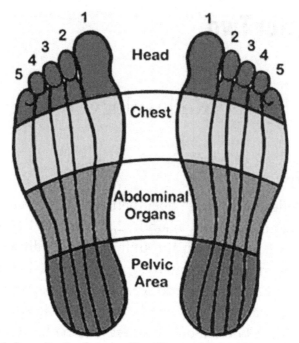

Figure 1. Longitudinal zones (Dr. Fitzgerald) and horizontal zones (Dr. Riley).

In 1903, after spending several years in London and Vienna, Dr. William Fitzgerald, a physician from Vermont, began researching the analgesic principles of Zone Therapy. He established that using continuous pressure in one area of the body could affect other areas. For example, putting a clamp on a finger provided enough analgesic effect to pull a tooth. In 1917, Fitzgerald wrote *Zone Therapy - Relieving Pain in the Home*.

Dr. Joe Riley, a student of Fitzgerald's, added horizontal waistline, midline, and diaphragm lines to the Zone Therapy map (Figure 1). The addition of the horizontal lines opened the door for Eunice Ingham, a physical therapist that worked for Dr. Riley, to create the first reflex map of the feet. She produced this map by scientifically testing Fitzgerald's research through documented trial-and-error work with Riley's clients. Using that scientific learning experience, Ingham created our modern-day version of the foot chart (Figure 2). This is the foundation from which all other foot charts have been generated. In 1938, Ingham wrote *Stories the Feet Can Tell*; it was translated into seven different languages and was responsible for introducing reflexology within and beyond the United States. Thirteen years later, she wrote her second book, *Stories the Feet Have Told*. Eunice Ingham is considered to be the founder of modern-day reflexology.

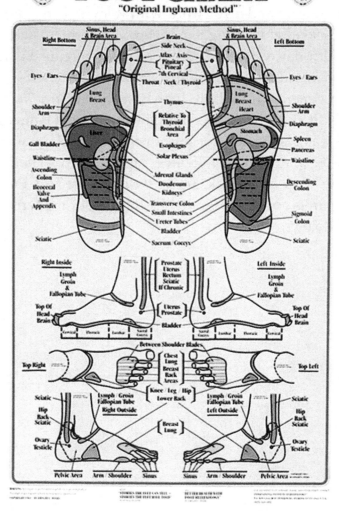

Figure 2. Eunice Ingham's Reflexology foot chart. Used with permission from the International Institute of Reflexology.

In 1968, Eunice Ingham and her nephew, Dwight Byers, formed what is now known as the International Institute of Reflexology. Byers picked up the torch from his aunt after she died in 1974 and continued her vision of promoting better health through holistic methods. In addition to operating the Institute, which is the oldest active reflexology school in the U.S., Byers authored *Better Health with Foot Reflexology - The Original Ingham Methodmu* in 1983. In his book, Byers introduced the map of the foot's reflection of the body, which is an important visual tool that dramatically impacts the ability to see the body through the feet (Figure 3). It was my good fortune to study reflexology and become certified under Dwight Byers in 1998.

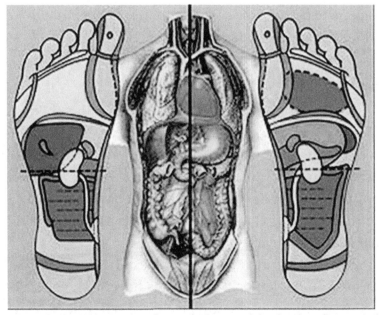

Figure 3. Dwight Byer's color-coded map of the foot's reflection of the body. Used with permission from the International Institute of Reflexology.

Reflexology has continued to evolve as we are now able to incorporate the benefits of modern clinical settings, systems, protocols, and education. The following definition of reflexology was agreed upon in 2015 by The Reflexology Association of America, The American Reflexology Certification Board, and The National Council of Reflexology Educators:

Reflexology is a protocol of manual techniques such as thumb and finger walking, hook and back-up, and rotating on a point, applied to specific reflex areas predominantly on the feet and hands. These techniques stimulate the complex neural pathways linking the body systems, supporting the body's efforts to function optimally. The effectiveness of Reflexology is recognized worldwide by various national health institutions and the public at large as a distinct complementary practice within the holistic health field.

Reflexology Techniques

Anyone practicing ERM must have the ability to identify where there are energy blockages in the foot reflexes. A good working knowledge of three reflexology techniques, three relaxation techniques, and the appropriate application of essential oils will enable the practitioner to create an effective wellness plan individualized for every client.

In some circumstances, reflexology can be performed on the hands. Hand maps have been generated and the techniques are similar to foot reflexology. However, the hands are not as sensitive or responsive as the feet and the practitioner must use more pressure for longer periods of time. Hand reflexology is explored further in Chapter 7 Self-care.

The three fundamental reflexology techniques are *thumb/finger walking, hook and backup,* and *rotating on a point. Thumb/finger walking* is the most widely used method. The thumb or any finger is placed anywhere on the foot, and brief pressure followed by brief relaxation is applied without losing skin contact (Figure 4). The resulting forward movement is a crawling motion similar to that of an inch worm. Each forward movement is called a bite. The goal of thumb/finger walking is to identify blockages in reflex points, sometimes referred to as crystals or deposits. Thumb/finger walking is also used to indicate the nature of a blockage (does it involve excess or deficient energy?) so that the proper release strategy can be applied.

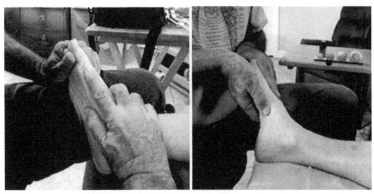

Figure 4. Thumb/finger walking technique.

The *hook-and-backup technique* is an advanced pinpoint process typically used for deep reflex points that are hidden under the tissue (for example, pituitary and pineal glands, ileocecal valve, appendix, and sigmoid colon). It is a three-step method (Figure 5) starting with the thumb walk taking small bites to reach the target reflex point (A), followed by a repositioning of the thumb to a 90 degree angle (hook; B). Finally, the thumb applies firm downward reverse pressure to the reflex (backup; C). These deep reflex points are the most tender and sensitive areas on the feet. Care and caution must be employed when using the hook-and-backup.

Figure 5. Hook-and-backup technique.

The third fundamental technique is *rotating on a point*. Using the thumb or a finger, firm circular movements are applied to the target reflex point (Figure 6). The first three rotations are counterclockwise on the outer edge of the reflex, and the next three rotations are clockwise directly on the reflex. This method is primarily used to break up crystals or deposits that are so thick they are blocking access to a reflex point. In addition, there are some reflexes (for example, the uterus, ovaries, hips, and knees) that respond particularly well to rotating on a point, regardless of the blockage condition.

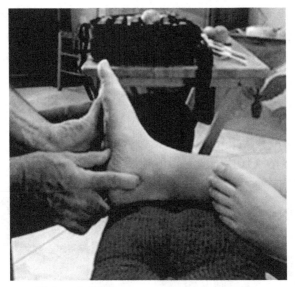

Figure 6. Rotating on a point technique.

Relaxation Techniques

Relaxation is used during an ERM session to accomplish three specific goals: 1) at the beginning of a session to calm the client and bring them into the present moment; 2) to help release discomfort after blockage has been removed; and 3) to finish a session on a positive, pleasant note. There are three key relaxation techniques in reflexology; hand position for all of these techniques is critical if the above goals are to be accomplished. Any of the techniques can be used at any time and the choice of technique will be dependent on your client's personal preference.

The first relaxation technique is *back and forth* or *side to side* (Figure 7). The center concave portion of the palm of each hand is placed on either side of the client's foot at the diaphragm line extended (i.e., the ball of the foot) (A). Gentle pressure is applied with both hands while loose contact is maintained. The foot is rolled from side to side between the hands in a gentle back and forth motion (B), with the hands quickly moving in opposite directions (C). This technique can be used for ten seconds up to a full minute on each foot.

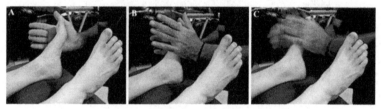

Figure 7. Back and forth or side to side relaxation technique.

The second relaxation technique is *ankle loosening* (Figure 8). The center concave portion of the palm of each hand is placed on either side of the client's foot directly in front of the ankle bones (A). The ankle is completely cupped within the hands. The hands use the ankle as a pivot point as they move backward and forward quickly, much like the motion made when trying to warm the hands (B). The foot will shake from side to side when the technique is properly executed. The motion should continue until the practitioner feels that the ankle is fully relaxed, 30 seconds up to a full minute.

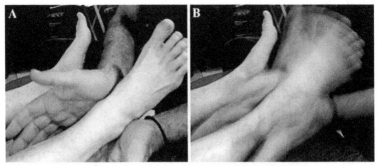

Figure 8. Ankle loosening relaxation technique.

The third and most relaxing technique is the *spinal twist* (Figure 9). Tilt the right foot outward, revealing and giving access to the entire spinal reflex (A). Grasp the foot from the inside of the instep with both hands as close to the heel as possible, with the fingers on top and the thumb on the bottom (B). The web between the thumb and index finger of both hands should rest directly on the spinal reflex. With the sides of the index fingers and the thumbs touching each other, the right hand (closest to the ankle) provides firm support while the left hand (nearest the toes) executes a twisting action, much like twisting a throttle (C, D). Both hands remain touching the foot during the process of twisting and moving up the foot.

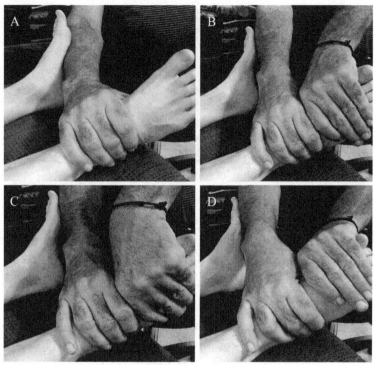

Figure 9. Spinal twist relaxation technique.

Reflexology is the cornerstone of the ERM wellness system. For the practitioner, all of the physical information you need to successfully treat your clients is found through reflexology. For the layperson, mastering a few techniques and understanding the maps and charts allow you to perform self-care and treatment of your family using ERM.

Chapter Three

Essential Oils

Essential oils are highly concentrated volatile oils that are distilled or cold pressed from plants. They retain the regenerating, protective, and immune-fortifying properties of the plants from which they are derived. Two important physiological components of essential oils are that their molecular structure is small and that they are fat-soluble. These characteristics enable the oils to penetrate the skin quickly and easily. Their fat solubility also allows the oils to pass through internal cell membranes so that they can potentially impact every cell in the body within 20 minutes of application. The use of essential oils for everything from pain relief to repairing bone and muscle damage, to emotional, mental, and spiritual applications has occurred for thousands of years.

Oftentimes, when a reflex on the foot is sensitive (indicating a blockage), the client will feel pain or be uncomfortable. A friend suggested that I try essential oils to relieve the pain and relax the client. Essential oils are effective because the feet have an abundance of nerve endings and the skin easily absorbs the oils. By applying the appropriate oil to specific spots on the foot, I open the reflexes and am able to determine the deeper nature of the congestion with less pressure and, therefore, less pain. As I studied more about the oils and worked with clients, my knowledge base grew as to what oils to use when. Oils became a very important part of the effectiveness of my FootGuy process. Although the primary use of essential oils in the practice of ERM is focused on the discovery component, essential oils can also be a powerful ending for an ERM session.

Knowing and understanding the basic characteristics and applications of essential oils provide a foundation of why they are a synergistic part of the ERM. There are seven essential oils that I use primarily: lemon, lavender, peppermint, frankincense, cedarwood, vetiver, and orange. The "Big Three", lemon, lavender, and peppermint, are the most versatile, are suitable for a myriad of circumstances, are easily used in combination with other oils, and are relatively inexpensive. No Foot-Guy session is completed without using at least one of these three oils. This table shows some of the common uses of the Big Three and is followed by a description of each.

Common uses of ERM's the Big Three essential oils.

Lemon	Lavender	Peppermint
sanitize	antioxidant	muscle and joint pain
anxiety	diabetes	sinus issues
depression	brain function	energy and performance

morning sickness	improves mood	headaches
pain	cuts	irritable bowel syndrome
cold symptoms	burns	bad breath
energizing	skin balance	scalp health
acne	hair health	itching
blood clotting	headaches	bug repellent
skin repair	pain	nausea
diuretic	sleep issues	acne
focus and attention	ADD – focus	sunburn

Lemon (*Citrus limon*) - The extraction method is cold-pressing the oil from the rind. Lemon affects the digestive, immune, and respiratory systems, and has exceptional antiseptic, antifungal, antiviral, and astringent properties. The primary emotional applications are to promote clarity of thought and a sense of well-being.

I use lemon for a wide variety of issues. Two common examples are on a congested kidney reflex, indicating the client is dealing with disappointment or failure, and on the throat reflex when the client's symptoms indicate an inability to speak up for themselves.

Lavender (*Lavandula angustifolia*) - The extraction method is by steam distillation of the flowers. Clinical studies conducted over the past 30 years overwhelmingly support the medicinal properties of lavender, particularly on the cardiovascular and nervous systems, and skin. The primary emotional applications are to relieve anxiety and to promote balance and calmness.

I use lavender at the beginning of every session to engender a sense of safety and trust.

Peppermint (*Mentha piperita*) - The extraction method is steam distillation of leaves. Peppermint affects the digestive, nervous, and respiratory systems, muscle, and bone. The primary emotional application is to soothe anger, depression, and hysteria.

I often use peppermint to relieve muscular tension in the neck by applying it to the reflexes on the inside of the great toe. Peppermint can also be used on the toe reflexes when anger at someone close to the client is indicated.

As a reflexologist, I could run my practice using only the Big Three oils. Most, if not all, of the physical challenges that a client experiences can be addressed by these three basic, yet powerful essential oils. However, ERM is more than just reflexology, and there are other deeper, non-physical applications for essential oils in the ERM wellness system. The following four oils help unravel the connections between what is being manifested physically by the client and the mental, emotional, and spiritual blockages causing the physical symptoms.

Frankincense (*Boswellia frereana*) - The extraction method is steam distillation of resin. Frankincense affects the immune and nervous systems, and the skin. The primary emotional applications are to provide emotional balance and relief from depression and indecision. It has many spiritual applications and is known as holy oil in several of the world's major religions.

A common phrase in the essential oil industry is "When in doubt, use Frank." I use frankincense on the spine reflexes to arouse nerve activity throughout the body, and on the brain reflex for head injuries or symptoms of depression or bipolar disorder.

Cedarwood (*Juniperus virginiana*) - The extraction method is steam distillation of the wood. It affects the nervous and respiratory systems; the primary emotional application is relief from anxiety and depression. Cedarwood is the Native American version of frankincense.

I use cedarwood in all of the ways I use frankincense, but also to relieve anxiety and to help center a scattered client.

Vetiver (*Vetiveria zizanioides*) - The extraction method is steam distillation of the root. Vetiver affects the hormonal and nervous systems and the skin. The primary emotional applications are for balance, grounding, and calming, and it can be used as a sedative.

Vetiver can be used alone, but it is also very effective when layered with other oils. For example, if a bipolar client comes to me in a manic state, I will layer vetiver and frankincense, in that order, to their spine and brain reflexes to calm the mania.

Orange (*Citrus sinensis*) - The extraction method is cold-pressing the oil from the rind. Orange affects the digestive and immune systems and the skin. Primary emotional applications are to uplift and stimulate and to provide emotional balance.

I layer orange on top of other oils to invigorate the client. A layering of frankincense and orange, in that order, down the spinal reflexes is my one-two punch against cancer.

A way to experience the synergistic effects of oils is blending. Two or more oils in varying ratios, depending on the intended use, are mixed together in a drip or roller bottle. A carrier such as mineral oil or jojoba oil may be added to help extend absorption time on the skin. My signature FootGuy blend is 4:1 orange to vetiver. I use it at the end of every session to leave the client feeling grounded, centered, uplifted, and ready to tackle life. Oil blends can also be mixed with water for use in a diffuser as an aromatherapy application. There are hundreds of essential oil blend recipes available on the internet for every imaginable circumstance or ailment.

There are three important practices that should be applied to the use of essential oils in ERM. The first of these is *sanitation*. The practitioner should always wash and sanitize the hands before a session begins. During the session, effective sanitation means eliminating contact between the essential oil bottle and the client's feet to ensure there is no contamination. Oil should be dripped onto the practitioner's thumb or fingers and applied to the client's feet so that the tip of the bottle never touches the practitioner or the client. Sanitation is crucial, so be vigilant.

The second practice, *application*, refers to where and why specific oils are applied to specific reflexes. This requires a merging of your knowledge of Ingham's foot chart, knowledge of your oils, and knowledge of the emotional body. The first step in effective application is the identification of the congestion of a reflex. This can be ascertained in two ways: 1) the practitioner feels crystals or deposits, or 2) the client reacting via a pain response to pressure on a reflex. The next step is using the foot chart to identify what body part is indicated by the location of the congestion on the foot. The body part then becomes the guide for which oil to use. The final step in the application practice is to incorporate the emotions; this step will be explored in Chapter 4.

Individual oils can be quite effective alone, but the third practice, *layering*, takes their efficacy to another level. Layering is when single oils are dropped one after another onto a reflex point. For example, layering equal amounts of lemon, lavender, and peppermint, in that order, on the adrenal reflexes of the feet creates a powerful barrier against the symptoms of allergies. Layering lavender and peppermint on the site of an insect sting reduces burning, itching, and swelling.

If essential oils interest you and you want to explore and use oils other than the ones discussed here, you need to study their attributes. Some oils are "hot" and can burn the skin if not applied properly. Additionally, some oils do not mix well with each other. Do your homework!

You have now been introduced to the fundamental reflexology techniques and the value of essential oils. The next step in the ERM process requires that you move out of your head and into your heart. Before there can be release of energy blockages that will lead to healing, emotional awareness must be included in order to fully understand the root causes of the client's physical health issues.

Chapter Four

Emotional Awareness

This chapter discussing emotions is the most important in this book. Incorporating emotions into the physical healing process is what sets ERM apart from other wellness systems. I have written this chapter primarily addressing the practitioner, but the layperson can also utilize emotional awareness to unravel their loved ones' physical issues. Where I use the word practitioner, just substitute layperson, and where I use client, substitute family member or friend. The layperson will not have to start from the beginning with their loved one; presumably you will have some idea of their existing emotional state. However, don't assume too much or you might miss discovering powerful hidden emotions that will shed valuable light on physical problems.

Identifying the physical indicators of blockages only addresses the symptoms of dis-ease, not the root causes. It has long been acknowledged that our emotional condition directly impacts our physical condition. A primary example of this is stress, one of the most devastating ailments in our world today. Another example is depression, which commonly manifests as irritability, trouble sleeping, and aches and pains throughout the body. A credible extension of this concept is that all of our physical ailments have an underlying emotional component. Understanding these components will assist the practitioner in putting together the client's entire story, leading them to balance.

So how does one go about discovering and helping the client address emotional issues that may not only be deeply personal, but also deeply painful? This is a multistep process that requires the practitioner to develop several atypical characteristics: 1) to be comfortable with their own emotions and those of their clients; 2) to model vulnerability so that the client does not feel threatened or intimidated; and 3) to recognize and trust their intuition. To be successful, the ERM practitioner must cultivate these characteristics from a heart space that truly believes that the emotions are the key to wellness. Let's address these characteristics individually.

1. **To be comfortable with their own emotions and those of their clients:**

This is the basic definition of emotional intelligence, which is the cornerstone of the emotional awareness component in ERM. Gathering and processing the significant events that have impacted your life will create empathy, compassion, and understanding for the impact of traumatic events in other people's lives. There are multiple layers in this discovery process. One layer is personal and can be accomplished on your own via methods such as meditation, self-help books, and classes. Another layer is addressed by joining applicable groups like Alcoholics Anonymous, Adult Children of Alcoholics, Narcotics Anonymous, men's or women's empowerment groups, various support groups, or churches. A third avenue for guidance to self-awareness is through one-on-one professional therapeutic services, i.e., therapy.

2. **To model vulnerability so that the client does not feel threatened or intimidated:**

In order to gain a client's trust, the practitioner must be willing to share his/her own unpleasant and traumatic experiences. The practitioner's choice to be vulnerable gives the client permission to do the same. Vulnerability automatically comes with the processing of emotional trauma that was discussed in the paragraph above. You cannot genuinely work through your personal issues without choosing to let others in.

3. **To recognize and trust their intuition:**

Intuition is the ability to understand something immediately, without the need for conscious reasoning. Some people are born with heightened intuitive awareness, but we are all capable of learning to read the clues that other people give us regarding their inner emotional state. The tools used to acquire this somewhat ambiguous skill feel like an oxymoron. They are studying, applying logic and reason, and utilizing a scientific method to solve a problem. Becoming acutely aware of what people are telling you, regardless of the words they say, is the first step. The secret is practice and you can practice on everyone you encounter, not just clients.

It is also important to look at your own life experiences, as explained in characteristics 1 and 2 above, to see how they influenced your own physical and emotional conditions. There are numerous resources to help you with this journey; some of my favorites are Louise Hay (www.louishay.com), Lise Bourbeau (www.lisebourbeau.com), and Annette Noontil (www.annettenoontil.com). Reading body language is another exceptional way of decoding emotions and a wealth of information is available online.

Becoming aware of and comfortable with your emotions will lead to your ability to help others do the same. It takes willingness and practice, but it is a very gratifying part of being an ERM practitioner. Below are two examples of using your emotional awareness to serve the client.

I had a new client who scheduled the appointment because she was curious about reflexology. As we started the session, I began making small talk to help her relax. She mentioned her work, but primarily talked about her family, the upcoming Mother's Day, and an upcoming family reunion. Once I started working on her feet, I noticed tightness in her ankles, which indicates a lack of self-nurturing. I then started thumb-walking across the toe ridge of her left foot. At the base of her fourth toe, I got a strong dull and achy pain response, indicating a deficiency of energy. The fourth toe on the left foot represents your primary relationship. I put together my clues: her focus on family, lack of self-care, and difficulty in her primary relationship. This led me to ask if she was having problems in her relationship with her husband and she told me they were in the middle of a divorce. While continuing to work that specific reflex on her fourth toe, I asked her some pointed questions (how long had the divorce process been going on, how did she feel about the divorce) so that she would express her emotions (I feel sad, I feel like a failure, I am angry). These are critical moments in the session, the time when the client acknowledges the emotional pain. She cried. Her hips and legs immediately relaxed and her ankles became flexible. For the remainder of the session, our conversation centered around her personal empowerment and how she could provide stability for her family. When she arrived at the session, she was very stressed and uptight, but by the time she left, she felt more confident and ready to better handle the issues and responsibilities that she was facing. I saw that as success.

This second session example is one of my favorites because I was wrong, and we always have to be ready and willing to be wrong in order to best serve our clients. A 35-year-old father and successful entrepreneur had been coming for sessions once every few weeks for several months. This time he showed up with acute lower back pain and I began to work on the spinal and hip reflexes. As our session conversation proceeded, he shared that he was having atypical sexual performance issues and that he was also being short-tempered with his children, which felt totally out of character. My first instinct, based on the clues of lower back pain, sexual performance issues, and irritability with loved ones, was to ask him about early childhood sexual abuse. He gave me a blank look and said he didn't recall anything like that, so I dug deeper. I asked him if there were times from when he was young that he didn't remember, suspecting that I would find evidence of repressed memories caused by severe trauma. He said that he remembered his entire childhood, sincerely expressing that, "We were poor, but we were happy." His father was a drug addict and had lost everything on several occasions, but the family always managed to pull through. I continued working on the spinal and hip reflexes and used some frankincense oil to make the reflexes more responsive. My next option was to take a different direction, so I asked him where in his life he was not feeling supported. He immediately said, "at work" and I realized that my first notion was wrong. His business partner, who was also his mother-in-law, had been micro-managing and second-guessing his every decision at work. He admitted to experiencing a lack of self-confidence caused by constantly being criticized, and was feeling serious resentment toward his mother-in-law. As I continued working the same reflexes, we discussed how these stressors were the cause of his back pain, sexual issues, and lack of patience. I suggested that he confront his mother-in-law and share his feelings, fears, and resentments, and although he was not excited at the prospect, he agreed to do it. At this point, I began working the shoulder reflexes and solar plexus reflexes on both feet to help him release his anger and anxiety as we discussed the desired outcome of the conversation with his mother-in -law. The next day, he talked with her and things went very well. She acknowledged that she had not been trusting him and was not even sure why. Their relationship improved and so did their business. The physical issues caused by his distress at work disappeared and life at home became much more pleasant.

In Appendix C, there is an important reference titled the Emotions Template. It lists a number of specific physical ailments and their corresponding emotional causes, and is a compilation from the work of Louise Hay, Annette Noontil, and Lise Bourbeau. After you practice ERM for a while, your ability to quickly intuit the client's emotions will improve, but in the meantime, the Emotions Template will be helpful. It also will provide options to explore when your original analysis is wrong. The Emotions Template is also discussed further in Chapter 6 Self-care.

I don't want to give anyone the impression that every ERM session is a profound, life-changing experience for the client. Sometimes there are no deep, distressing issues to be addressed, and occasionally the client falls asleep as soon as they sit in the chair. It is important to remember that the client is the healer and you are the facilitator helping the client come back to balance. We don't get to decide exactly what that looks like or how it occurs.

Chapter Five

Release

Welcome to Release, the goal of the work accomplished in the ERM process. This final step allows the body the freedom to move back to a place of balance and wellness. The client's physical issues have been discovered and the emotional attachments that contribute to the physical ailments have been identified and acknowledged. Releasing those attachments for many people is difficult because their story is how they identify themselves, some since childhood.

The modern-day tools of tuning forks and Wellness Spheres are used to relieve physical pain and release the blocked emotions. This chapter introduces the value of these multipurpose tools for use by the practitioner and layperson, as well as demonstrates how the tools can empower clients to participate in their own healing.

Tuning Forks

Although tuning forks were created hundreds of years ago with the advent of musical instruments such as the piano, in the healing arts they are a relatively new tool. It has only been in the last few decades that vibrational and sound medicine has gained recognition as a viable component of the wellness industry. Tuning forks range in size from one-inch forks that sound like Tinkerbell to forks that are 22 inches long and have deep resonating tones.

I use two specific forks in ERM: the Sun (126.22 MHz) and the Moon (210.42 MHz). These two forks are the closest vibrational representation of the needle manipulation techniques practiced in acupuncture; they can help bring blocked reflexes back into balanced harmonic resonance by infusing or diffusing energy. In ERM, the Sun and the Moon tuning forks are used to realign the vibrational equilibrium of the entire body through the reflexes of the feet. The choice of which tuning fork to use in any given situation, the Sun or the Moon, is based on the revelations you have gained from working with your client. When a reflex is out of balance and the reflex pain experienced is dull and achy, a deficiency of energy is indicated. In order to achieve balance, energy must be infused by applying the Sun tuning fork to the reflex. Conversely, if the reflex pain experienced is sharp and shooting, there is excess energy associated with the reflex. The Moon tuning fork is used to diffuse the level of energy. During the application of the tuning forks, it is important to revisit the emotional aspects that the client has consciously or unconsciously divulged to you. The combination of purposely addressing the physical and emotional components of the client's illness or discomfort will effectively encourage the release that must occur before wellness can be achieved.

The following instructions show how to activate a fork using an activation puck, how to properly hold a tuning fork, as well as when and where to use tuning forks.

Step 1 - Activation: Hold the tuning fork at the base of the tines between the index finger and thumb, with the stem encompassed in the palm of the hand by the other fingers (Figure 1). Strike one side of the tines on the activation puck or any solid surface.

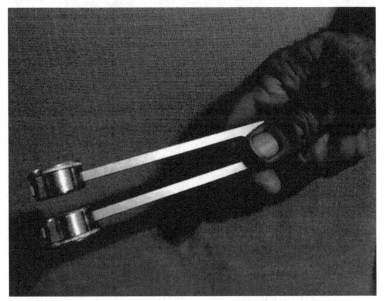

Figure 1. Proper way to hold a tuning fork.

Step 2 - Application: There are three tuning fork techniques used in ERM to relieve physical discomfort and facilitate the release of blocked emotions:

1. The first is Direct Reflex Application. After activation, the base of the stem of the tuning

fork is placed directly on top of the reflex being treated (Figure 2). There is a multitude of pinpoint reflexes with corresponding emotional concerns that can be addressed with this technique.

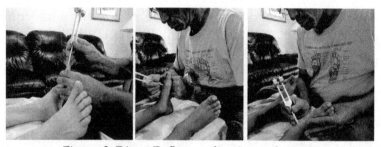

Figure 2. Direct Reflex application technique.

2. The second technique is Stem Application. After activation, the stem of the tuning fork is laid flat across the region of the foot needing attention (Figure 3). One example of this is to lay the stem along the bottom of the ankle bone to relax the ankle and address issues of the lymph reflexes (A). Another example is to place the stem along the muscles between the great toe and the second toe, reducing the pain and structural deformities of a bunion (B). Both lymph issues and bunions are correlated with a lack of love and joy for the experiences of life. Balancing the energy in those reflexes releases the emotional blockage and allows the client to move beyond their negative patterns.

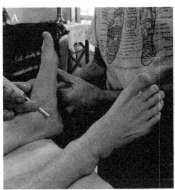

Figure 3. Example techniques for Stem Application
of the tuning fork.

3. The third technique is Sliding Stem Application (Figure 4). After activation, the stem of the tuning fork is laid flat at the base of the spinal reflexes. The fork is then skimmed up the foot along the spinal reflexes until the top is reached (A). The tuning fork is then reactivated and the process repeated in reverse, starting at the top of the spinal reflexes and moving to the bottom (B). There are 26 different reflex points located along the spinal reflexes, each with a correlating emotional element.

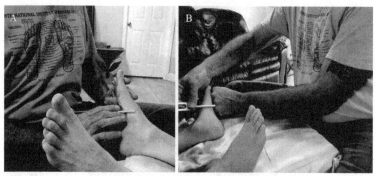

Figure 4. Sliding Stem Application

Tuning forks in ERM are key to achieving energy balance, just as the needle in acupuncture augments or reduces qi (energy). By paying attention to the clues given by your client during the reflexology portion of the session, you can determine how to apply the right fork at the right spot to get the best result.

The original intention for the Sun and Moon tuning forks was to tune the energy throughout the entire body. Many conditions can be addressed with an energy tuning, including ADD, ADHD, anxiety, nervousness, mild bipolar symptoms, brain fog, and focus and concentration issues. Any complaint that involves brain imbalance would benefit from a whole body Sun and Moon tuning fork treatment. The method for this technique is explained in Appendix D.

Wellness Spheres

Most of the intense emotional release work in ERM is done with tuning forks. Wellness Spheres are used to complete the release, and to smooth and calm the emotions. I created Wellness Spheres in 2016 as a therapeutic tool not only for client use by practitioners, but for client self-care as well. They are the final phase of the release process and of this wellness system. This set of four ½-inch to 1 ¼-inch wooden balls is designed to address all of the reflexes of the feet (Figure 5). The smaller Spheres can be used to pinpoint specific spots, while the larger Spheres cover the entire foot to smooth the energy that has been realigned during the session. Because they are made of wood, Wellness Spheres last a lifetime, and are easy to clean and maintain. The Spheres can be personalized with the client's favorite essential oils. When displayed in their tray, the Spheres are both visually appealing and readily available for use. Wellness Spheres are portable and can be carried by clients to their sessions, to their home for self-treatment, or anywhere the client wants to engage in self-care.

Figure 5. Wellness Spheres

The Wellness Spheres sizes were chosen so that all of the reflexes on a wide variety of feet would be accessible. Below are examples of uses for each of the Sphere sizes. Refer to Ingham's foot chart (Chapter 2) for locations of the reflexes on the feet.

1. ½-inch - This Sphere works well on small feet, and on tight regions of any sized foot. Typical reflexes that respond to the ½-inch Sphere are arms, shoulders, ears, eyes, neck, and the bronchial line. In addition, this Sphere was created to access pinpoint spots such as the ileocecal valve and appendix reflexes (Figure 6).

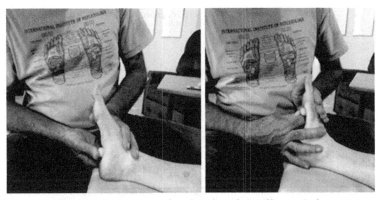

Figure 6. Applications for the ½ inch Wellness Sphere.

2. ¾-inch - This Sphere is used on the heel to impact the sigmoid colon and the sciatic (Figure 7, A) and on the interior ankle to impact the uterus and prostate (B). It is also used on the ball of the foot to affect the lungs, heart, and chest.

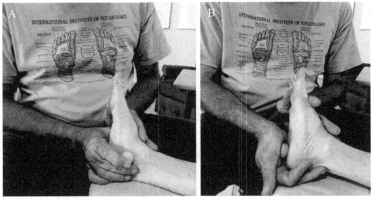

Figure 7. Applications for the 3/4 inch Wellness Sphere.

3. 1-inch - This Sphere is used on the arch of the foot and addresses all of the core body components

from the diaphragm down to the pelvic line (Figure 8, A).

4. 1 ¼-inch - This Sphere addresses everything that the 1-inch Sphere does, but it is intended for large feet. It is also the main tool for dealing with plantar fasciitis (Figure 8, B).

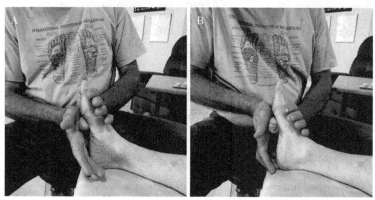

Figure 8. Applications for the 1 inch (A) and
1 ¼ inch (B) Wellness Spheres.

There are two methods for using Wellness Spheres. First, hold the Sphere in the palm of your hand and roll it against the plantar surface of the foot in an up-and-down (Figure 9, A) or side-to-side (B) motion. Use the thumb of your other hand as a guide to keep the Sphere on the foot. This method is used for all of the Wellness Sphere techniques except pinpoint applications.

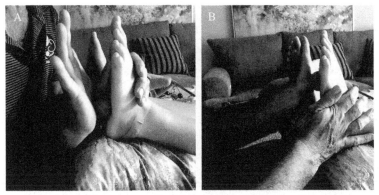

Figure 9. The two methods for using Wellness Spheres.

The second Wellness Spheres method uses only the ½-inch Sphere and is for pinpoint applications. Instead of rolling the Sphere with the palm of the hand, the fingertips and thumb push the Sphere directly onto the reflex (Figure 10). This compression technique not only gives access to the pinpoint reflexes, it can also be used in areas where rolling a Sphere is not possible, such as in between the toes.

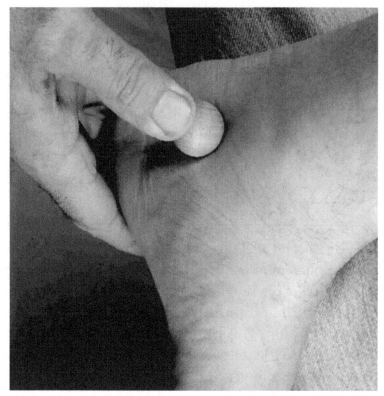

Figure 10. The pinpoint application of Wellness Spheres.

There are two aspects of using oils with the Spheres. One is sealing the Spheres with an essential oil and mineral oil mixture that protects the Spheres from wear and contamination. The essential oil chosen for this use can be anything applicable to the client's emotional needs, such as insomnia, anxiety, or memory loss. The other use of essential oils with the Spheres is direct oiling. Instead of the traditional application of oils from the bottle to the practitioner's hand to the client's foot, oil is dripped onto the Sphere while it is being held on the foot and then rolled across the reflexes (Figure 11). Again, the oil chosen can be suitable to facilitate the specific emotional release needed. Over time, the addition of various essential oils onto the Spheres creates a synergistic effect that is unique to each client.

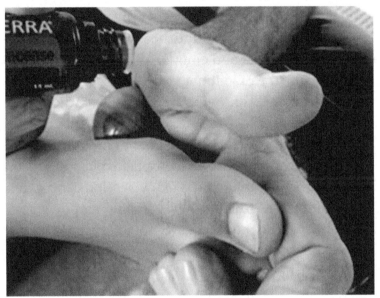

Figure 11. Dripping oil onto a Sphere for direct application.

When used by a practitioner on clients, the Spheres should be cleaned after each session with a mild soap and water and then air dried. They will need to be re-sealed with a blend of mineral oil and essential oils after every ten clients. Proper consistent care will help your Wellness Spheres last for a long time!

Tuning forks and Wellness Spheres are powerful tools that help facilitate the release of blocked emotional energy that is vital to achieving lasting wellness. The

Sun and Moon tuning forks can be used to infuse or diffuse energy from specific reflexes, or to balance the energy of the entire body. Wellness Spheres also release stagnant energy through a combination of the absorbing qualities of the wood, the opening and softening effects of the essential oils, and the rhythmic, calming motion of the Spheres on the reflexes. Not only can the wellness practitioner use these multipurpose tools to help clients address the physical and emotional components of their illness or pain, the practitioner can also teach clients how Wellness Spheres can empower them to participate in their own healing.

The release of blocked, stagnant emotions leading to physical health might be accomplished in one session. For some clients, it may take many sessions and a genuine commitment to their own personal empowerment and wellness. The practitioner is not just the provider of the tools; the practitioner is also the witness and guide for their journey.

Chapter Six

Putting It All Together

Let's walk through a typical ERM session. What do you do; what should you notice; and what can you say to successfully guide your client to balance and healing? The process below is written for work with a new client. This same basic structure can be used with friends or family. If a new client becomes a long-term client, you can modify the process to fit your relationship. However, it is important to remember not to become too comfortable with your long-term clients. You don't want to miss clues or overlook issues, and there is always room to go deeper.

Before the Client Arrives

The session actually begins when the person contacts you for an appointment. At that moment, they are going to tell you why they want your help. Pay attention. This is your first clue for best serving this client. Next, they will tell you how they found you; if they don't mention that, ask. Clients referred by other clients will arrive at their session with the expectation of being helped. Clients who found you online or through other means of marketing are searching for a solution to a physical ailment and will arrive expecting nothing more than that. The difference between the two is subtle. The client that is referred will be easier to help because they *expect* to be healed; the other client *hopes* to be healed. If you are a practitioner, get the client's contact information so you can send them an intake form (Appendix B). Ask them to return the completed form or bring it with them to the first session. What you learn from that form will help you decipher what happens during the session.

Once the Client Arrives

When the client arrives, exchange pleasantries, and look over their intake sheet if it was not sent to you earlier. Help the client get into the chair. This first seating of your client is important because it allows you to create the feelings of care, nurturing, and safety. Make sure they are positioned properly so that they are comfortable and that their feet are raised enough to be easily accessible. Sit down, drip four drops of lavender on your hands, and wash it over the client's feet.

Discovery

Next, take their feet and place the bottoms of them on your chest, look the person in the eyes, and ask, "Why are you here?". You are encouraging the client to tell you their story, their view of life, and the various people and circumstances that affect them. You might have to prod a bit to get more than a superficial response. It is often beneficial at this point to begin the three reflexology relaxation techniques (Chapter 2) that will help the client settle in and share. Ask short, directed questions and then shut up and listen. Really listen, using the intuitive skills you have developed. The details of the client's story are not important, but what they are revealing is the lens through which they view their world. This is now the time to begin the reflexology techniques explained in Chapter 2, working the entirety of the feet, but focusing on those reflexes that correspond to what you have learned.

This is when you really get busy! Like a duck appearing to swim gracefully on top of the water, you are paddling like crazy underneath. As you accumulate the details of their condition, you must also be creating the solution in your mind. These are the questions to ask yourself, while continuing to pay attention to your client's words: Are the reflex points and pressure you are using appropriate for what you are hearing? What are the reactions to what you are doing (is there a pain response)? When there is a reaction to a reflex stimulation, what is the corresponding body part? What are the emotions associated with that body part (see the Emotions Template Appendix C)? Which essential oils can be applied, based on the physical and emotional clues, that would help you go deeper into the discovery process (Chapter 3)?

In the midst of this complicated discovery scenario, you are using the reflexology and oils to verify your hunches as to what emotions are really causing the physical pain. Once you have gathered your information based on their reactions (don't get caught up in the drama of their story), it is time to tell them what you suspect is the underlying cause of their discomfort. You may be right, but you must also be willing to be wrong. If the client convinces you that your suspicions are incorrect, consider other alternatives that might also explain their situation based on the emotions template. If you cannot determine an emotional correlation with the physical issue or the client will not admit a connection, continue on to the Release segment of the session so you can bring the physical reflex back into balance. Establishing the emotional connection is a difficult phenomenon to explain and it will not happen every time with every client.

Owning the Emotions

If you make progress with the client's acceptance of their emotional situation, ask them to agree or disagree with what you have observed. This gives them the opportunity to admit and own their uncomfortable emotions and embrace their shadow side. There may be tears or anger or a quiet understanding of the truth. It is important that they accept their discomfort, even for just a moment, and really feel it. Once they face their shadows squarely, they have an awareness of what has to be released and they are ready to move on to the next step.

Release

Tuning forks are the tool of choice in this moment. Using the pain response descriptions discussed in Chapter 5, either the Sun or the Moon tuning fork is chosen to bring the reflexes back into balance. Doing a second reflexology run over the feet to check on the previous tender spots is helpful. You can use the tuning forks on the areas that are still out of balance. Wellness Spheres are the final tool used in the Release portion of the session. Rolling the Spheres over the specific areas of the feet that have been stimulated helps calm the reflexes. Rubbing the entire bottom surface of the feet with a Sphere is incredibly relaxing and helps the client accept and move beyond any physical and/or emotional discomfort they may have felt. For long-term clients who have their own Spheres, their favorite essential oils can be applied to the Spheres to further personalize their effectiveness. Wellness Spheres help the client mentally absorb the session experience and encourage feelings of empowerment.

Closing the Session

To end the session, put four drops of FootGuy blend oils (see Chapter 3) on your hands and wash the client's feet. Next, go through all three of the relaxation techniques explained in Chapter 2. After you finish, the client may need a few moments to pull themselves together. When they are ready, bring the chair to the upright position and help them stand up. Before they leave, set a follow-up appointment (when necessary) and give them any homework that you feel is appropriate to assist them on their journey.

Now you have a general idea of what a full ERM session entails. Of course, every client is different, and you should not expect to always follow this outline rigidly. Be aware, be flexible, and practice, practice, practice.

Chapter Seven

Self-care

This chapter is for both laypeople who want to learn how to take care of themselves, their families, and their friends, and the professionals who want to teach self-care to their clients. Each of the five components of ERM (reflexology, essential oils, emotional awareness, tuning forks, and wellness spheres) has aspects that can be perfected by anyone willing to take the time and make the effort to become empowered. The self-care aspects of each of these tools are detailed below and if you learn to consistently use any or all of them, your life will be positively impacted.

Reflexology

Reflexology for self-care presents some challenges. You must be able to sit in a chair and get your foot onto your lap. Even if that can be accomplished, not all of the reflex points can be accessed. Until now, I have only discussed reflexology treatment on the feet. However, the hands also have reflex points that can be used, and the hands are much more accessible for self-care. Hand reflex points correspond to the same areas of the body as the reflex points in the feet, but are not quite as sensitive; you have to compress the hand reflexes more often and with more force. The techniques for working on the hands are the same as those used on the feet that were described in Chapter 2. The beauty of using the hands is that you can work on them at any time and place. Remember to be aware of your body's reactions to the work because that will be important later when it is time to release or infuse energy. The chart below (Figure 1), produced by the International Institute of Reflexology, shows the reflexes of the body as they are laid out in the hands. There are many similar charts available, but I use this one because it was developed by Eunice Ingham, the creator of modern day reflexology.

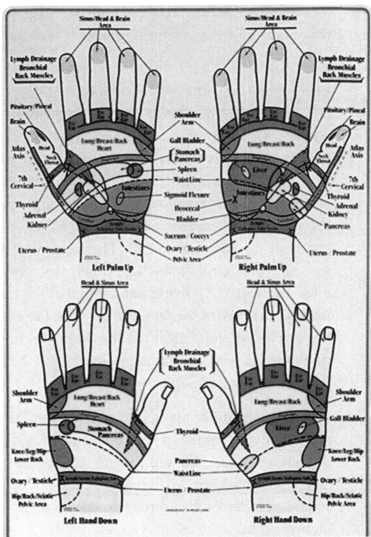

Figure 1. Reflexology hand chart. Used with permission from the
International Institute of Reflexology.

Essential Oils

Essential oils are incredibly powerful self-care tools that can be used in a variety of ways, and they have become commonplace in the wellness industry over the past few years. Here are some simple guidelines for their use:

- Instructions for using oils commonly say to apply oils all over the bottom of the feet because they will quickly be absorbed. While it is true that the feet are quite pervious, it is more effective to rub a couple of drops of a specific oil directly onto the target reflex. An excellent example is applying lavender to the adrenal reflexes on the feet and hands of a hyperactive child. The frequency of the oil will almost immediately help the child relax and focus. Applying peppermint along the ridge at the base of the toes and between the toes helps relax tension felt in the shoulders. Putting frankincense on the spinal reflexes will help relieve anxiety and depression.

- Essential oils can be applied to many other parts of the body to both help with tension or various discomforts, such as on the neck, shoulders, and lower back, or to change one's emotional state. Lavender rubbed directly onto the temples induces calm relaxation. Vetiver on the pulse points is very grounding. A mix of peppermint and lavender helps reduce inflammation. Be careful not to touch the eyes, mucous membranes, or other sensitive areas with the oils.

- The oldest and most widely recognized application of essential oils is aromatherapy. The energy or tone of an entire space can be set by picking the right oil to infuse. For example, infusing lavender can induce relaxation, while infusing any citrus oil will invigorate and energize. Diffusing peppermint will help clear sinus congestion.

- Roller bottles are small bottles with a roll-on tip that are easy to use and will fit in a pocket or purse. A single oil or a blend of two or more oils is mixed with a carrier, such as coconut oil. The carrier holds the essential oil on the skin so that the fragrance lasts longer, and it dilutes the essential oil so it can be used more often. A roller bottle application of any citrus oil will get you through the mid-afternoon energy slump. The FootGuy blend (wild orange and vetiver) is both invigorating and grounding, perfect for the classroom or office. Creating your own personal blend of oils that you find calming can be invaluable for helping when anxiety strikes. Roller bottles can be very empowering because your specific wellness issues can be addressed easily with your own unique solution.

- There are large multi-level marketing essential oil companies such as DoTerra and Young Living that provide vast amounts of information and opportunities. There is an endless supply of oil recipes and projects in multiple online web pages. Shared events such as classes and parties are popular and can promote a healthy lifestyle within the community.

Essential oils are an amazing wellness tool, but remember that they are also very powerful. Educate yourself and use them responsibly.

Emotional Awareness

Emotional awareness is the aspect of ERM that sets it apart from other wellness modalities. Based on the premise that physical ailments have an emotional origin, becoming aware of one's toxic emotions, accepting them, and letting them go enhances the body's ability to heal and achieve balance. In this section, I discuss three ways to increase your emotional awareness: grounding, using an emotions guide, and mirror work.

Before engaging in any self-care, and especially if you are caring for others, it is important to become grounded. Grounding allows the energy that comes from the people and situations around you to move through you safely. You become centered and present, aware of your surroundings. You become aware of yourself physically and emotionally. Grounding creates a firm foundation for any challenging emotional work that you may need to do or help someone else process. Also, any excess energy that sticks to you after doing emotional work needs to be released before you move back into your life. In the following chapter, Homework, I go into more detail on grounding and explain a number of grounding techniques.

The Emotions Guide in Appendix C is a concise list of physical conditions and their corresponding emotional causes; it is based on the work of Louise Hay, Annette Noontil, and Lise Bourbeau. The use of the Emotions Guide for self-care is different than when it is used by a practitioner with a client (see Chapter 4). The practitioner is working to discover the story that the client is trying to convey, either consciously or subconsciously, based on their physical reactions to the reflexology. A person that is caring for themselves or a family member already knows where there is pain and discomfort. They can go straight to the emotions guide to determine the emotional meaning or cause of the physical pain. The next step is to verify that the meaning is accurate by asking if what the emotions guide is suggesting is the truth. Oftentimes, our first reaction to this question will be "no", but if that happens, dig deeper, look objectively at the situation, and be completely honest with yourself. If you are working with someone else, encourage them to do the same. Once the emotional cause is discovered and accepted, the corresponding reflex from the Emotions Guide is stimulated on the foot or hand (see the foot chart in Chapter 2 or the hand chart above). Notice the type of pain response elicited from the reflex stimulation because it reveals more about the nature of the physical issue and the emotional cause. For example, a sharp and shooting pain caused by stimulating the neck reflex on the hand indicates a reluctance to see or appreciate another's point of view. Once the information is gathered, and here is the beauty of using the emotions template for self-care, you can immediately begin to improve your well-being by taking an applicable affirmation from *Heal Your Life* by Louise Hay and making it part of your daily self-care routine. Repeat the affirmation until you believe it and the pain will be relieved and balance will return. This process using the emotions template is particularly successful for people who have already realized that the circumstances in their life are causing negative emotional and physical impacts, and are willing to own their story and move past it.

Another emotional awareness self-care tool that was developed by Louise Hay is mirror work, detailed in her book, *Mirror Work: 21 Days to Heal Your Life.* Following the daily exercises and using the affirmations is a powerful beginning to what can become a life-long practice of loving yourself. Mirror work teaches you to stop disliking (or even hating) your image and shows you how to make the mirror your best friend. You will grow a deep, intimate relationship with yourself that will serve you regardless of outer circumstances or the opinions of others. This is the first step to harnessing the toxic emotions that are at the root of your physical challenges.

Release

Once the physical and emotional blockages causing pain are discovered and acknowledged, they can be released by infusing or withdrawing energy. ERM uses two specific tools, tuning forks and Wellness Spheres, to accomplish the energy balancing. Both of these tools are well suited for self-care and caring for others.

The Sun and Moon are the tuning forks used in ERM to balance the energy and relieve the discomfort that is revealed during the reflexology session. When the pain from stimulating a reflex is sharp, like being poked by a piece of broken glass, striking the Moon tuning fork on the puck and touching the vibrating handle to the reflex point releases excess energy. When the pain from stimulating the reflex is dull, like a bruise from stepping on a stone, striking the Sun on the puck and touching the reflex infuses energy. This not only works on the reflexes on the feet and hands, but also on muscles throughout the body.

The energy field of the entire body can be smoothed by following the traditional tuning fork technique outlined in Chapter 5 (Release). The balance created by the Sun and the Moon together can help with ADD, ADHD, focusing issues, depression, bipolar disorder symptoms and more. One does not need to become a trained tuning fork expert to benefit from using the Sun and Moon on themselves and others. Energy field smoothing can be done as part of a morning grounding ritual, as daily support for anxiety or depression, to help become centered before taking tests, or prior to taking part in athletic events. Using tuning forks in this manner has multiple therapeutic, personal performance, and lifestyle applications. Tuning forks are especially good for children and teens when they need to become centered and focused.

Wellness Spheres are the most versatile tool in the ERM wellness system and are particularly suited for self-care. They can be used on hand and foot reflexes or on any sore or tense muscles on the entire body. You can use them on yourself or on another person, including the elderly or children. Refer to Chapter 5 (Release) for instructions, and the following pictures illustrate a variety of ways to use Wellness Spheres.

On your own feet:

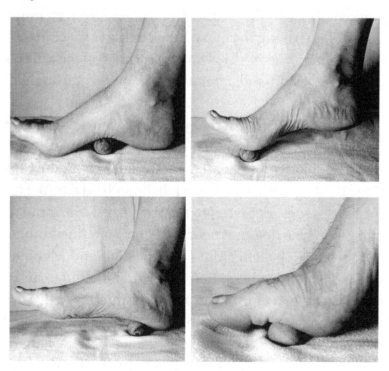

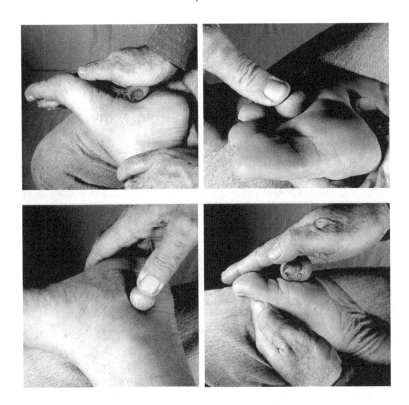

On your hands:

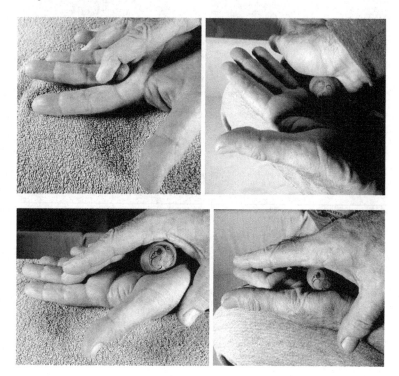

On someone else's feet:

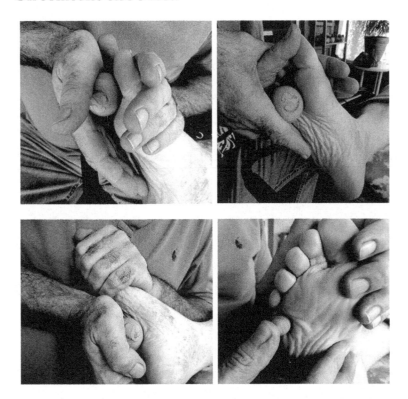

These are some of the different ways that Wellness Spheres can be applied in your life as both a self-empowerment and self-care tool, allowing you to take an active role in your own wellness and health. The beautiful thing is that you don't really need to be an expert - just do it and the benefits will speak for themselves.

Chapter Eight

Homework

After 20+ years of being a reflexologist and 30+ years of facilitating emotional work, I have learned that none of this can be completely understood by attending a class or reading a book. Experience is the best teacher. The following tidbits are things that I have gathered along the way and want to share to make your path easier, more efficient, and lots more fun! There are two sections: Grounding and Self-care Homework. I have put Grounding into its own section because I believe that it is a non-negotiable aspect of healing yourself and others. In addition, I strongly urge everyone that ventures into ERM, both the practitioner and the layperson, to engage in the self-care practices. As a practitioner, having had the emotional experiences invoked by these assignments is an important piece of the trust relationship you develop with your client. Whether you have been a wellness practitioner for many years, are new to the healing arts, or are a layperson interested in only helping yourself and your loved ones, these tips will guide you in a direction that will support your process.

Grounding is exactly what it sounds like: connecting yourself to the planet. For eons, humans walked barefoot or wore foot coverings that did not impede the natural electromagnetic connection between their body and the living earth. With the advent of concrete, asphalt, rubber-soled shoes, above-ground living, high-speed rail, and air travel, we have separated ourselves as a species from the planet. Now we must make a conscious commitment to reestablish and maintain that natural organic electromagnetic connection that is so vital for all aspects of the human condition. So the question becomes: How do we accomplish this in the society and culture that we exist in today? Grounding should be done intentionally and consistently every day. The following examples and ideas can be used to create your own grounding practices, and I must reiterate that grounding is an absolute must for your own well-being and that of anyone in your care.

The objective of grounding is to bring yourself back into the present moment. There are many easy, enjoyable things you can do in the course of a day that will ground you. These activities include:

- Walk or stand barefoot on the earth - pretty basic!

- Bounce - Use a trampoline or small rebounder. This activates the lymph system and opens the reflexes in the feet, creating a grounding response in the body.

- Hold a Sacred Object - Choose a small item that makes you feel relaxed or empowered. It can be a special stone or crystal, a sentimental piece of jewelry, anything you love and that brings you joy. Hold it in your hands, tune into the energy, and breathe.

- Hand in Water - Go to a sink, turn on the cold water, and place your right hand on top of the faucet with your fingers in the water. Hold the intention that all of the negative energy within you is being released through your right hand into the water which flows down the drain and out of your house.

- Eat Protein - Red meat is particularly effective because it is dense and digests slowly. Consuming large portions of red meat frequently is not particularly healthy, but when occasionally used, it can be a powerful grounding tool.

- Sex - There is nothing like good, authentic sex to bring you into the moment and connect you with another human being.

- Yoga - requires focused, intentional breathing and concentration on body movement; very grounding

- Martial Arts - just like yoga, except with more intensity

- Dancing - Put on the music and connect with it, move with abandon, and don't worry about how you look. Feel the music and go.

- Foot Focus Meditation - Sit quietly with eyes opened or closed. Bring your attention to both baby toes. Next, allow that concentration to move out to cover both feet. Ask yourself these questions: Where are my feet? (Are they on the sand, in a pair of dress shoes, in the tub?), and How do my feet feel? (Are they hot, cold, sore, comfortable?). Once your attention is completely absorbed into your feet, take a few deep breaths and release your anxiety or negative emotions into the earth through the bottoms of your feet.

- 5,4,3,2,1 Meditation - Sit quietly and find 5 things you can see with your eyes, 4 things you can hear with your ears, 3 things you can feel, 2 things you can smell, and 1 thing you can taste. Do this entire meditation with your eyes open and become present in your environment. This can be done quickly and discreetly, or you can spend as much time as you desire.

- Feel the Chair Meditation - Sit quietly on a comfortable, supportive chair, eyes opened or closed. Ask yourself: Where do I feel the chair? Can I feel it on my upper back, middle back, lower back, butt? Is the chair soft, hard, springy, warm, cold? Do I feel the chair supporting me? Breathe. Accept the support and fall into the chair. Feel your body relax and become one with the chair. Enjoy!

There are several things you can do to help you make grounding a way of life. These are:

- Create a sacred space in your home for doing rituals and meditating.

- Learn some simple grounding exercises that can be done anywhere, anytime of the day or night.

- Create grounding rituals, chants, or prayers that reflect your personal intentions and desires.

- Spend time outside so that you can make a deep connection to the living breathing planet that you walk upon.

- Do a 21-day challenge. It takes at least 21 days to develop a habit, so commit to doing a grounding technique for that length of time. It will change your life.

Grounding is all of this and more. Grounding combats the depression and regret that come from spending time on past negative circumstances, and it combats anxiety which results from worrying about the future. The act of grounding brings us back to the present moment. It also allows us to support others, primarily children, to reduce negative kinetic energy explosions, hyperactivity, mental frustration, and attention issues. Stage fright, deep loss, grief, and other life moments when being present is essential can be positively impacted by grounding. Whether you are 7 or 70 years old, these tools are tried and true, easy and effective.

Self-care Homework

These tips are for practitioners to use for themselves and to give to their clients, as well as for laypeople who want to enhance their own well-being and that of their loved ones. I have practiced them repeatedly for many years. They are part of my spiritual walk and my self-care habits, and are much of the reason that I am successfully guiding people through the ERM process. Take a look at them all and choose to explore whatever speaks to you. I do suggest that practitioners first try the exercises themselves that they intend to assign to their clients.

- Mirror Work - This homework is given during a session when a client has a new, more positive response to an old emotional trigger - an "ah ha" moment. As soon as it happens, I ask them to check in with how they feel, immediately go to a mirror, look into their own eyes, and feel it. What this does is open the client to explore their new awareness (the "ah ha") and to internalize the positive feeling that comes with it. The homework is to remember to choose that good feeling over their old conditioned emotional response when presented with the negative trigger.

- Journaling - This homework is given to someone who is stuck in their drama story or a specific traumatic event. I first ask them if they are willing to commit to 15 minutes of time every day for 14 days. Once they agree, I explain the details: 10 minutes of journaling each morning before getting out of bed immediately followed by 5 minutes of listening. Listening consists of 100% concentration on everything you can hear with your eyes closed. That's it, every day. The 10 minutes of writing supports two processes: 1) it assists the natural ability of the subconscious to unravel dreams, leading to a release of the story, and 2) putting the story down in writing on a piece of paper gets it out of the client's head. The listening portion becomes more profound over time as the client realizes what they can actually hear in the world around them when they are not replaying their pain over and over in their mind.

- Empowerment - This homework is for people who constantly belittle and put themselves down. I tell them this story: There is a little girl and her dad on Facebook that have a beautiful morning ritual. The little girl was with her mom, who was a heroin addict, for several years before coming to live with her dad. Her self-esteem and self-love were gone. So, every morning, first thing, he stands her up on the bathroom counter and she says to the mirror, loudly and boldly, I am strong, I am beautiful, I am smart, I am bright, and other empowering statements. When she is finished, Dad lifts her off the counter and she starts her day. When I give this homework, I ask them to do the same ritual themselves (without necessarily standing on the counter) for 21 days. This process will reprogram their mind and their self-talk will become empowering instead of destructive. It takes a minimum of 21 days to form a new habit, but in reality this can be forever homework for all of us!

• 1-5-10 Meditation - This is another 21-day homework exercise that I give to people who insist they can't meditate. On Week 1, meditate for one minute a day. Week 2, meditate for five minutes a day. Week 3, meditate for ten minutes a day. The directions for meditation are: sit in a comfortable chair, completely open your body with feet on the floor, close your eyes, and focus all of your attention on your breathing. When you are distracted, return to focusing on your breathing. As with the Empowerment exercise above, meditation can be valuable forever homework for all of us.

• Affirmations - Affirmations are different from empowerment statements because they are very specific and intentional. I have Louise Hay's book *Heal Your Life* downloaded on my tablet. During a session, when I find a reflex point that is out of balance, I look up the corresponding affirmation, give it to the client, and tell them to repeat it five times a day for at least five days while looking in a mirror. When affirmations are used, they help the client release the emotional imbalance indicated by the reflex response. This homework is good for just about anyone and the affirmations can be tailored to every situation when a new outlook or attitude is wanted.

* Breathwork - This homework is for people who suffer with anxiety. It is a cyclical process: breathe in for 6 seconds, hold it for 3 seconds, breathe out for 6 seconds, hold it for 3 seconds. Repeat the cycle 5 times or until the anxiety diminishes.

* Rebounder - This is a physical assignment that is specifically for those with lymph issues. A Rebounder is a 3-foot diameter trampoline that sits 8 inches off the ground. Rebounders are readily available in stores and online. Place the Rebounder, handle side out, against a wall. Step onto the center of the Rebounder, placing one hand on the handle and the other hand on the wall. Bounce for 10 minutes in the morning and 10 minutes at night. While bouncing, your feet should not leave the trampoline surface. The light bouncing helps stimulate the lymph system, relieving physical symptoms such as ankle and leg swelling and edema throughout the body.

* Michael Jackson - This exercise will help with calf and heel pain and plantar fasciitis. Find a parking lot that has the triangular-shaped parking bumpers at the front of the parking spot. Facing the bumper, place both feet on one side with your heels on the ground and your toes stretching toward the top. Lean your body over the top of

the bumper, keeping your back straight. Do this 3 times every time you get the chance for as long as it takes to relieve your pain.

- Lion King - This is for people who have forgotten who they are and feel like they have no purpose. Those who best respond to this homework are on two ends of a spectrum: they are extremely logical and see the world in black-and-white, or they are more impulsive and see the world in rainbows. I tell them to go home and watch the original animated version of the Disney movie, The Lion King. This movie is effective for such opposite personality types because it gets the logical people out of their heads, and the animation and music reach impulsive people that are shut down. I tell them to pay particular attention to the scene where the mandrill, Rafiki, and the lion cub, Simba, are in the field together. Rafiki shows Simba, by whacking him on the head with his staff, that he must acknowledge his past so that he can step into his future. I have found this homework to be very cathartic for many people.

- Walk and Pray, Sit and Listen - This exercise is from Buddhist warrior training and is excellent for people who are struggling spiritually or want more discipline in their life. I tell them to pray, and to walk while they are praying. When their prayers are complete, they sit down and listen for exactly half the time that they prayed. This can create a very disciplined practice over a long enough period of time. Anyone who is searching for something to improve their spiritual journey will benefit from this homework.

Chapter Nine

Personal Empowerment

Healing is serious, strenuous business, and caregivers must be cognizant of their own well-being as well as their clients'. By recognizing more than just the physical aspects of a session and being aware of the energy produced by the client and caregiver, a much more enhanced, effective outcome can be obtained. Energy Medicine is the concept that a vital energy controls the processes of our bodies. Health and healing come from manipulating the flow of that energy to balance the body's electromagnetic field.

Here are several practices that I follow to keep my clients and myself centered and focused:

- Permission - Practitioners must always have permission from a person to work on them. This ensures that their personal space is respected and that they are engaged. This is important to prevent you from overstepping your bounds.

- Who's the Healer? - Remember that you are guiding your client in their process of healing. They are the healer; you are the facilitator.

- Fan Blades - People are like a 4-bladed ceiling fan with each blade representing 1 of 4 distinct energy fields: the physical, mental, emotional, and spiritual. These fields come together with the heart at the center to form a human being. All of the blades must be in alignment, or the fan runs poorly because it is out of balance. Your job as a practitioner is to keep all four of your blades in balance so you can help your clients do the same.

- Where Two or More are Gathered - When ERM is practiced well, there is an amazing phenomenon that happens in the growing relationship you build with your client. It is an energetic synergy that can best be described by the old Biblical terminology of "where two or more are gathered". Once the practitioner and the client are physically touching, the energy circuit is closed. That flow of energy allows connection of the emotional, mental, and spiritual bodies to the physical, enhancing every aspect of healing that is possible. This phenomenon is difficult to explain and must be experienced to be appreciated.

- Breathwork - There are three scenarios where breathwork can be quite helpful to the practitioner. 1) During a session, if you begin to feel overwhelmed, use a 4-2 breath - breathe in for 4 seconds, hold it for 2 seconds, breathe out for 4 seconds, and hold it for 2 seconds. Repeat as needed to reduce anxiety. 2) If during a session you notice that your client needs to breathe, remind them. Intentional breathing will help them better process emotions, and they won't pass out. 3) When your client is struggling with a traumatic memory, align your breathing with theirs. The synchronistic rhythm of both of your breaths will assist their movement through the experience.

• Body Quadrants - The body is divided into 4 sections, each with specific characteristics. The right half represents masculine energy and the left half, feminine energy. The half above the waistline represents regrets and resentments from the past and the half below the waistline, fear of the future. Every pain in the body will occur in at least two of the sections. Assessing the characteristics of those sections will provide insight into the client's story and the root of the imbalance.

• Healer's Reflection - I have noticed that I often attract clients that want help with issues I am working on myself. It's an interesting phenomenon, so be aware, and when it happens, don't miss the lessons.

Chapter Ten

Business Options for Practitioners

I am a reflexologist, an ordained minister, a teacher, a workshop facilitator, an author, and an inventor. I've been a short-order cook, a restaurant manager, and a bartender, too. I'm not a business coach or a business consultant, yet. I do, however, see the possibilities in the ERM model I created, as well as what could be done by separating this wellness system into its component parts. Point being, the creation of multiple revenue sources can be an effective way of generating profits and building community. When you give people several reasons to engage, you begin to really get to know them, and they know and trust you. Let's explore some of the ERM system options.

- ERM as a Stand-alone Wellness System - This is how I operate The FootGuy, LLC, mobile reflexology service using the entire ERM system.

- ERM as a Stand-alone Offering Within Your Practice - If you have already established yourself as a bodyworker, healer, or therapist, and you want to expand your client base, this system is fully accessible as soon as you are trained and certified in ERM. This option is a particularly good fit for a holistic wellness center or practice.

- ERM Split into Its Individual Parts - This system can be divided into its five main pieces (reflexology, essential oils, emotional awareness, tuning forks, and Wellness Spheres) and each can be offered as a stand-alone therapy. This adds great depth to your practice and creates options using any combination of the five pieces, as well as adding other modalities to the mix. The result is the ability to produce a personalized wellness plan for your clients.

- ERM Tools for Self-care - Essential oils, tuning forks, and Wellness Spheres can be sold as self-care tools that clients can purchase to use at home. Each tool has training classes that you can offer so clients learn to use the tools effectively. This creates revenue and grows your wellness community.

Revenue Sources

The following companies and concepts are additional revenue streams that I use to support and supplement The FootGuy:

- DoTerra is a multi-level marketing (MLM) company that produces the essential oils I use, as well as other home and health products and nutritional supplements. You or your clients can purchase products directly from DoTerra or from a distributor such as The FootGuy. You can also become a distributor to take advantage of wholesale pricing and provide an additional revenue stream. There are several other reputable essential oil companies that you can investigate, such as Young Living and Pure Haven.

- Voxx Socks is also a MLM company. They produce high performance technology socks that help with balance, mobility, energy, and pain management. As with DoTerra, you or your clients can purchase products directly from Voxx or from a distributor such as The FootGuy, or you can become a distributor.

- Sun and Moon tuning forks can be purchased by practitioners wholesale through The FootGuy. I also offer a very affordable 2-hour class online to teach you how to use them. By the end of the class, you will be certified to teach clients and students to use the Sun and Moon tuning forks for taking care of their families and themselves. I purchase my tuning forks from Medivibe; you, too, can purchase directly from them and become a distributor.

- Wellness Spheres and a 2-hour online certification training are available from The FootGuy. Once you are certified, you will have the knowledge needed to teach your clients and students how to use the Spheres to foster and maintain wellness for themselves and others.

Conclusion

Emotive Reflex Method - Ancient Healing for a Modern World is a multifaceted book. It is a book of instruction to teach readers the basics of a number of different healing modalities. It is a book of action with many "to dos" that will reinforce the teachings and take the learning to a higher level. Most importantly, it is a wellness empowerment tool that, once read and absorbed, will inspire people to treat their clients, loved ones, and themselves with care and reverence.

The two audiences for which ERM was written, wellness professionals and laypeople, have different intentions and reasons for practicing ERM. However, the implementation of the various pieces is the same. You have to be willing to study and learn the body work so you can be proficient doing basic reflexology and using essential oils, tuning forks, and Wellness Spheres. You also have to develop your emotional superpowers: empathy, vulnerability, fearlessness, and understanding. When these characteristics are strong, your intuition becomes reliable and valuable. Self-care is another important piece of the formula, not only for teaching clients and loved ones, but first and foremost, for yourself. This work is not easy, but it will make your healing capabilities extraordinary.

Don't expect to do this work alone. Every individual has their own strengths; discover yours, but don't let your ego keep you from relying on others. I never could have developed ERM on my own. Find teachers and mentors, ask questions, and listen carefully to suggestions with an open mind. Consider whatever feedback may come your way. Find or build your own wellness community.

To my fellow wellness professionals, it is my hope that you will embrace wellness empowerment and client self-care. To the laypeople that are venturing into these practices, I hope that you will adopt healthy lifestyle choices and personal wellness responsibility.

Finally, please don't forget that we facilitate healing and that the people we care for are really the healers. It's always an inside job.

Next Steps

If you found this book to be enlightening and you are inspired to dig deeper, here are some products that can support your journey:

www.emotivereflexmethod.com

- Emotive Reflex Method – soft cover book
- Emotive Reflex Method – Kindle book
- Emotive Reflex Method –Master Trainer Program home study course
- Emotive Reflex Method – Master Trainer Program in-person class schedule

For those who want to explore blocked or disowned emotions, we offer a breakthrough workshop called "The Way Through Experience." This powerful, life-altering weekend has taken place in central Florida for the past 30 years. It is the foundation for the emotions work that underpins ERM.

www.thewaythroughexperience.com

www.thefootguy.rocks

- Purchase Wellness Spheres or become a Wellness Spheres affiliate
- Purchase DoTerra Essential Oils

- Purchase FootGuy foot care products or become a FootGuy affiliate

If you live in or visit the Florida Space Coast area, you can make an appointment for a session with Scott Donat, the FootGuy, at www.thefootguy.rocks.

Appendix A

Early Reflexologist Dr. Mahlon Locke

In 1905, during the same time that *Zone Therapy* was being introduced in America, a physician named Mahlon Locke graduated from Queen's University in Ontario. He went to Edinburgh, Scotland, to do his postgraduate training for two years, returning to Williamsburg, Ontario, where he purchased his medical practice. One of Dr. Locke's talents was foot manipulation, and it is unclear as to whether he learned his techniques in Scotland or from Native Americans living in his town. Locke's first patient was the local blacksmith, Peter Beckstead, who was unable to work because of his fallen arches. Locke manipulated Beckstead's feet and instructed the local shoemaker to construct a small cotton pillow insert for Beckstead's shoes. This was the first known instance of the use of orthotics. Over his 33-year career, Locke treated tens of thousands of people, working on 200 - 300 people a day. He would manipulate the feet for between 10 and 60 seconds per person and then move to the next client. A session cost $1 and people from all over the world came to see Dr. Locke. Some clients would experience immediate healing and others would require multiple manipulations. When Locke began his practice, there were 300 residents in Williamsburg. Over the years, two hotels and multiple shops and restaurants were built around his practice location, and the economy of the small town exploded.

Locke had his own health issues and died in 1942 from a stroke at 61 years old. Although his son and brother-in-law claimed that Locke had trained them, they could not reproduce his remarkable results and the clinic soon closed. Locke left no writings to explain his methods or techniques and when he died, all of his knowledge died with him. Dr. Locke's story and the opportunity he missed to leave an amazing legacy were a major motivation for me to write this book. When we make a discovery or create something new, it is imperative that we document and share the knowledge. ERM is a truly incredible wellness tool and it is my hope that this book will give the healers coming behind me a hand up.

Dr. Malhon Locke, the Toe Twister

Crowd lining up at daybreak to see Dr. Locke.

Appendix B

ERM Client Intake Form

(The electronic, fillable version of this form is available on www.thefootguy.rocks.)

Date_____

Name_____

Age_____

Address_____

_____

Phone_____

Email_____

Circle all that apply:

Single   Married   Divorced   Widowed

Daughters_____   # Sons_____

What makes you happy?

_____

_____

_____

_____

_____

Things that you are most proud of:

_____

_____

_____

_____

_____

Diagnosed Illnesses:

_____

_____

_____

_____

_____

Medications:

_____

_____

_____

_____

_____

Current (within last 6 months) pain, discomfort, or other health issues (circle all that apply):

Migraines	Sinuses	Teeth
Ears	Jaw	Neck
Shoulder	Chest	Upper Back
Middle Back	Lower Back	Hips
Knees	Calves	Ankles
Feet	Respiratory	Stomach
Abdominal	Gastrointestinal	Kidneys
Bladder	Liver	Spleen
Colon	Menstrual	Prostate
Skin	Muscle	Blood
Anxiety	Insomnia	Eating Disorder

Other Illnesses or Issues:

_____

_____

_____

_____

_____

Appendix C

ERM Emotions Template

(The electronic, fillable version of this form is available on www.thefootguy.rocks.)

Condition	Emotional Correlation
Migraines	not living one's true nature; feel guilty for questioning authority; sexual relationships issues
Sinuses	repressed anger; provoked
(Nose)	difficulty taking in life; fear of own or others suffering; distrust; fear; difficulty adjusting socially
Teeth	fear of making incorrect decisions; feel unable to defend oneself
Ears	judgmental about what you are hearing; internal anger; difficulty listening to others

(Hearing loss)	stubbornness; closed to the advice of others; fear of disobeying
(Pain)	guilt; punishing oneself
(Tinnitus)	noisy mind; fear loss of self-control
Jaw	repressed anger; difficulty tackling life
Neck	inflexibility in thinking; not in control; concerned with what might be going on behind your back
Shoulder	emotionally burdened; sacrifice self for others
Arms	not doing enough for yourself; doubt one's usefulness
Hands	(right) afraid to give or (left) afraid to receive
Chest	lack of love for or from family
Back Pain	do not feel supported
(Upper)	emotional insecurity

(Middle)	fear of material loss
(Lower)	fear of losing freedom or life
Hips	difficulty or fear of moving forward in life
Knees	inflexible, especially about the future
Calves	fear of moving forward too quickly
Ankles	fear of moving forward or in a different direction
Feet	difficulty finding the means to move forward in life
Respiratory	depression
Stomach/Abdomen	resist new ideas; fear of failure
Gastrointestinal	prolonged uncertainty; feeling of doom
Kidneys	poor judgment; trouble making decisions; over-emotional

(Disease)	perceived lack of inner resources; life isn't fair
Bladder	related to yearning
(overactive)	rigidly control desires; afraid to acknowledge desires
(incontinence)	inability to control desires; lack of judgement; want immediate gratification
Liver	repressed anger; sadness; bitterness
Spleen	obsessive concern or worry; discouraged; overwhelmed; emotionally empty
Colon	inability to let go of what you no longer need
Menstrual	difficulty accepting your femaleness; subconsciously prefer to be male
(heavy bleeding)	loss of joy in your life

Prostate	sense of powerlessness; weariness; inability to surrender control
Skin	shame and self-depreciation; keep others at a distance
(skin cancer)	bitterness from being rejected
Muscle	lack of motivation or willpower to fulfill desires
Blood Disorders	difficulty managing life; overly dramatic, emotional, and reactive
Anxiety	inability to live effectively in the present based on concerns caused by the past, producing worry about the future
Insomnia	inability to move past unresolved issues or circumstances

Eating Disorders

(anorexia)

rejection of feminine;
obsessed with perfection;
cut off from feelings

(bulimia)

hate mother; confusion
regarding femaleness; fear
abandonment; prevent
self from getting desires

Appendix D

Whole Body Tuning

The original intention for the Sun and Moon tuning forks was to tune the energy throughout the entire body. Many conditions can be addressed with an energy tuning, including ADD, ADHD, anxiety, nervousness, mild bipolar symptoms, brain fog, and focus and concentration issues. Any complaint that involves brain imbalance would benefit from a whole body Sun and Moon tuning fork treatment. The method for this technique is explained below.

Step 1. Activate one of the forks and sweep it from the ground on one side of the body (left or right) over the top of the head and back to the ground on the other side, holding the fork approximately three inches away from the body (pictured below). Repeat with the other tuning fork.

Step 2. Activate both forks at the same time. Place the Moon fork beside the left ear and the Sun fork beside the right ear and hold them there until the vibration has ended.

This technique is used to bring the masculine and feminine polarities of the physical and emotional bodies into alignment. The response will be immediate and calming, and will result in mental clarity, emotional stability, and focused intention.

Appendix E

Resources

- Reflexology – www.reflexology-USA.net
- Essential Oils – www.TheFootGuy.Rocks
- Emotional Awareness – www.thewaythroughexperience.com
- Tuning Forks – www.universalenergymassage.com
- Wellness Spheres – www.emotivereflexmethod.com
- Shannon Procise, CEO, Business Acceleration Network (small business management, marketing, community building) – www.businessaccelerationnetwork.com
- Robert Raymond, CEO, Achieve Systems (online coaching, business vision support, Achieve University) – www.achievesystempro.com

About the Author

- Last drink so far on February 7, 1986. One day at a time.

- The Way Through Experience (emotional breakthrough workshop): participant in September 1991, co-leader 1992 - 1995, lead facilitator since 2000

- Men's work facilitator: 1992 – 1997

- Certified Reiki practitioner: 1993

- Certified hypnotherapist: 1994

- Co-owner Synergy Center of Brevard (alternative health clinic): 1995 – 2003

- Certified reflexologist: since 1998

- People of Diversity (spiritual community): member since 2006, board member since 2020

- Founder and owner of The FootGuy, LLC: since 2014

- Ordained minister: since 2014

- DoTerra Essential Oils affiliate: since 2015

- Wellness Spheres creator: 2016

- Achieve Systems member: since 2016

- Voxx Sox affiliate: since 2017

- Reiki Master: since 2017

- Emotive Reflex Method Master Trainer System creator: 2018

Scott Donat has a unique combination of life experiences and formal education that has led to his path of helping people confront and conquer their physical issues and emotional demons. He endured difficult childhood circumstances, including being homeless and an alcoholic by age 16. After taking his last drink in 1986 and spending several years working the steps in Alcoholics Anonymous, Scott became a participant in The Way Through Experience, a weekend-long emotional breakthrough workshop. It so changed his life that he has continued his involvement with The Way Through and eventually became the lead facilitator. Scott was co-owner of an alternative health clinic from 1995 through 2003 where he was introduced to many of the healing techniques he uses today, including being certified as a reflexologist in 1998. After leaving the clinic, he practiced reflexology sporadically while raising his children and earning his living working in the restaurant business, holding every position from server to cook to manager and owner. In 2014, after a particularly frustrating and unfulfilling period in his career, Scott became a full-time reflexologist and started The FootGuy, LLC. It wasn't long before he realized that healing from reflexology was so much more effective and long-lasting when the client's emotional issues were brought into the mix, and Emotive Reflex Method was born.

Scott and his wife, Becky Bolt, live in Cocoa, Florida. Besides their real jobs, they help administer their multifaith spiritual community, People of Diversity, and continue to facilitate the Way Through Experience workshops. Between them, they have four daughters, ten grandchildren, and a busy, enjoyable life.

Made in the USA
Columbia, SC
01 November 2021